Railways in Profile Series

BRITISH RAILWAY WAGONS

OPENS and HOPPERS

Compiled by G. Gamble

CHEONA PUBLICATIONS

ISBN 1 900298 01 5

Production, design and setting by
Print-Rite, The Willows, School Lane
Stadhampton, Oxford OX44 7TR

Printed by Alpha Print, Crawley, Oxon

Published by
Cheona Publications
39 The Avenue, Chinnor, Oxfordshire OX9 4PD

Preface

This book sets the scene post-nationalisation by showing some of the inherited freight vehicles at work on British Railways and also illustrates some of the new wagon designs launched into service by BR. It is intended to act as an aid to modellers and also others who need photographs to assist in the assembly and alteration of the many plastic/etched brass/cast kits now available. As much detail as available has been put into the captions of the photographs but to save repetition, livery details are those given in the introductory section unless otherwise stated. These can generally be resolved into fitted (vacuum braked stock) or unfitted, where braking was independent on each wagon and could not be controlled by the driver or guard when the train was in motion. It is not possible to cover all wagon types in one book, so other volumes in the series are intended to cover vans, tank wagons, later BR stock, special and privately owned/leased stock as well as volumes on stations, lineside structures, signalling etc.

If you have material for any of the proposed volumes then please send it to the publishers for consideration.

G.Gamble
July 1996

Acknowledgements

Such a work as this relies heavily on the availability of photographs and so grateful thanks are extended to all who have made such material available to me. They have been indicated by initials and are: E.B - Eric Bruton, B.D. - Brian Daniels, G.E. - Gordon Eckersley collection, R.C. - Roger Carpenter, H.F.W. - Frank Wheeler (*via* Roger Carpenter), N - Nelson collection (courtesy Colin Judge), C.C. - Cheona collection, G.G. -. Geoff Gamble, B.R./A.B. - British Railways (A.Beaton collection), A.B. - A.Beaton collection, P.B. - Peter Bossom, T.R. - Tim Rogers and W.C. - Woods Collection (via Roger Carpenter). I would also like to thank Colin Judge for his help in the design and production of this book.

Introduction

On 1st January, 1948, the 'Big Four' (Great Western; London Midland and Scottish; London and North Eastern and Southern Railways) were nationalised to form British Railways.

The new body inherited thousands of freight vehicles of varying designs from the 'Big Four' as well as a large number from private owners. Moves were soon made to commence scrapping the inherited stock and replacing it with standard designs because the old wagons were, in many cases, in a poor state of repair. Many of these vehicles had been used excessively during World War II when there was little time or money to service and repair them. Brakes on many of the vehicles were inefficient, restricting the speed at which freight trains could travel and many wooden bodied vehicles had damaged timbers.

A repair programme was instituted alongside the new build - in many cases the latter involved merely changing diagram and lot numbers on batches of pre-grouping designs already going through the works.

In 1951, new standard designs began to appear - in many cases very similar to the pre-grouping ones but with improved brakes and running gear. There was also a move to replace the wooden body designs by steel ones. New designs appeared for the new traffic being developed, although the real assault on new wagon types took place in the late 1960's in an attempt to overcome the increasing momentum of loss of traffic to road transport.

The stock taken over by British Railways was re-numbered and new freight colours began to appear. Both of these operations took time to implement and indeed many of the inherited vehicles only had a new number painted on them and they were scrapped before being re-liveried.

15 years into BR and this typical scene features a variety of the standard wagon designs introduced post-1948. Ex-GWR Collett, class 28XX, No. 3848 shedded 86E (Severn Tunnel Junction), is seen on a down freight at Ruabon on 8th August, 1963.

The 28XX is hauling a rake of loaded 16T steel end door mineral wagons, like B67012 (coupled to the passenger luggage van on the right). In the foreground part of the interior of a 13T wooden bodied open wagon M422710 is seen coupled to a S & T Department ex-Sleeper wagon with rounded ends. Behind these two wagons stands a rake of empty Palbrick A wagons (note the two different ends visible on these wagons). Just ahead of No. 3848 a Shock open wagon with a sheet rail (vertical white stripes on the body) is coupled to a sheeted open wagon and some standard goods vans.   N.

Headlamp/Disc

The diagrams illustrate the arrangements of headlamps or discs used to indicate each class of train. This standard code was used on all British Railways steam locomotives and diesel shunters. It was also used on main line diesel locomotives and diesel multiple units before they were fitted with panel indicators. The system did not apply to Southern Region or Inter-Regional cross-London freight trains.

Under the modernisation plan a new system was evolved based on Western Region practice where a 4-character headcode was used in an indicator panel (where fitted). 2-character codes had preceded the 4-character ones.

Steam locomotives never had such panels fitted and the nearest they came to such a system involved the use of a small board with the train describer numbers on it, fixed to the top lamp iron on the front of the locomotive. This was only in common use on excursion trains.

Standard Train Class Code

Class

1 Express passenger train, newspaper train or breakdown van train; snow plough on duty; light engine proceeding to assist disabled train.

2 Ordinary passenger, branch passenger or 'mixed' train; breakdown van train not on duty.

3 Parcels, fish, fruit, livestock, milk or other perishable train composed entirely of vehicles conforming to coaching stock requirements; empty coaching stock (not specially authorised to carry Class 1 code).

4 Express freight train pipe-fitted throughout with the automatic vacuum brake operative on not less than 90 per cent of the vehicles.

5 Express freight train with the automatic brake operative on no fewer than half the vehicles.

6 Express freight train partly fitted with the automatic brake operative on not fewer than 20 per cent of the vehicles.

7 Express freight train not fitted with continuous brake.

8 Through freight train not fitted with the automatic brake.

9 Pick-up branch freight or ballast train requiring to stop in section

0 Light engine(s) with not more than two brake vans.

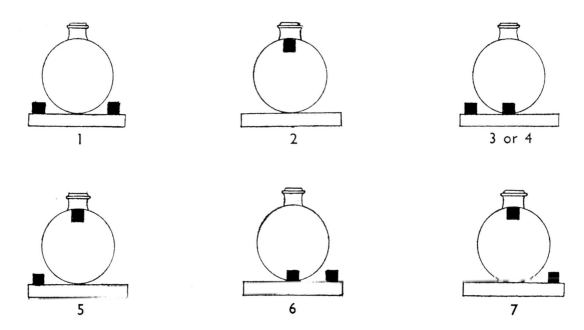

| 1 | 2 | 3 or 4 |

| 5 | 6 | 7 |

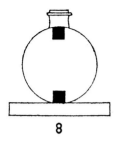
8

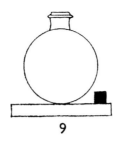
9

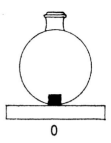
0

The following photographs illustrate the headcodes in use on freight trains which are the subject of this book. It should be noted that the 4-character headcode became a very complex system which has been admirably covered in the book entitled British Railways Headcodes - an Ian Allan ABC written by M.R.Bailey, but at this time long out of print.

1. Class 3 train. Ex-GWR 'County' Class, No. 1023 *County of Oxford* on a down milk train at Patchway station on 4th May, 1952.   N.

2. Class 4 train. Ex-GWR 'Castle' Class, No. 5063 *Earl Baldwin* with a Wolverhampton to Paddington stores and parcels train entering Birmingham Snow Hill on 16th April, 1964. N.

3. Class 5 train. Ex-GWR 'Hall' Class, No. 5999 *Wollaton Hall* on an up freight at Dunstall Park near Wolverhampton Low Level on 22nd June, 1961. N.

4. Class 6 train. Ex-GWR 'County' Class, No. 1013 *County of Dorset* on an up freight at Croes Newydd South Fork Yard on 18th April, 1963. **N.**

5. Class 7 train. Ex-LMS Stanier Class '8F', No. 48422, southbound with a train of 4-wheel oil tank wagons at Chirk on 2nd April, 1964. **N.**

6. Class 8 train. Ex-GWR Churchward Mogul, No. 6342 on a down iron ore train at Warwick on 20th August, 1956.   N.

7. Class 9 train. Ex-Caledonian Railway Pickersgill 4-4-0, No.54469 on a Perth local goods working at Blair Atholl on 2nd June, 1959.   N.

Diagram and LOT numbers

British Railways introduced three diagram books to cover freight stock. Book 1 was for ordinary wagons, Book 2 for specially built wagons and Book 3 for containers. The pages in each book were numbered from 1 and thus a wagon with a diagram number 1/108 would be found on page 108 of book 1.

The same diagram was often used to build batches of the same design of wagon over a period of time and by different builders so a lot number was allocated to each batch built i.e. Diagram 1/108 Lot 2223 - a batch of 500, 16Ton end door wagons with all steel welded body, numbered B70400 to B70899 and built by Birmingham Railway Carriage and Wagon Company in 1950.

Note: Diagram, Lot and Running numbers have been given wherever possible but the reader is reminded that variations did occur within a particular lot in some cases.

Numbering

Pre-Grouping Company Stock - retained the original number but this was prefixed by a single letter from the original company letters, (the latter were still retained on the original builder's plates but only the appropriate single letter was picked out in white).

Ex-GWR stock adopted the prefix letter		'W'
Ex-LMS	"	'M'
Ex-LNER	"	'E'
Ex-SR	"	'S'

Privately Owned Stock - was given the prefix 'P' followed by a number from 1 to 399999 allocated in a random fashion.

British Railways Built Stock - for general use had the prefix 'B' followed by a number selected from a batch allocated to the particular class of vehicle involved.

British Railways Built Stock - for the Engineers' department used the prefix 'DB'. Stock transferred from general use to this department was given the 'DB' prefix on the body - often before the original number which was retained on the original wagon plate on the solebars.

Liveries

Non-Fitted Stock - (not fitted with vacuum brakes) was given a grey body, black solebars, headstocks and below with a black or grey roof (where fitted). Lettering was in white on black panels.

Fitted Stock - (vacuum braked) was painted bauxite (a red/brown colour) for the body with black solebars, headstocks and below and a black or grey roof (where fitted). White lettering was applied directly onto the bauxite.

The original colours did vary, especially the grey, with the dust, rust and general grime of service much altering the base applied colours.

It should be noted that there was great variation in the painting of the chassis - sometimes the solebars were painted the same colour as the body and similarly the headstocks - this was more commonly seen on the fitted stock.

Insulated Stock - for the conveyance of perishables like fish and meat was painted white with black lettering. In 1957 this body colour was changed to a pale blue colour - ice blue, and white lettering was applied instead of the black.

Surprisingly there were anomalies here - banana vans were initially bauxite red whilst early batches of meat vans had body colours of light stone and crimson lake with yellow lettering (passenger stock livery). The latter livery was initially applied to non-insulated containers - fairly soon to be replaced by bauxite. Insulated containers followed the same livery patterns as insulated vans.

Engineers' Department Stock - was initially painted black with yellow lettering. This was later replaced by an olive green body colour.

Lettering - was similar to the style used from the 1930's by the pre-grouping companies. The number was painted on the lower left part of the body. If the vehicle had a code name this was painted above the number.

On the lower right of the body the tare weight was often noted. The solebar (the side frame of the chassis) carried the wagon plate and also, as appropriate, a builder's plate and a repairer's plate. The former plate was generally to the left and often close to it, would be the clip to hold the wagon load label, which was removed when the wagon reached its destination.

In the late 1950's all the lettering was grouped together at the lower left of the wagon side and it was surrounded by a white line.

As BR standard wagon designs were introduced telegraphic code names were issued but they were seldom used. Some of the names used were; PIPE, TUBE, PALVAN, SHOCVAN and later VANWIDE and VANFIT

TOPS - from 1972 the TOPS (Total Operations Processing System) was introduced where every vehicle on BR was given a computer recorded number and a 3-letter code. This system enabled an exact log to be kept of how many vehicles there were on the railway and their whereabouts.

TOPS Numbering - each wagon had its own fleet number, which if it was a new generation privately owned vehicle was preceded by capital letters derived from the name of the owner to clearly characterise it.

TOPS Code Letters

1. The first letter identifies the wagon type:-

> B = Bogie bolster, plate and rail wagons.
> C = Brake vans, covered hoppers and gunpowder vans.
> F = Flat wagons including carflats, conflats and freightliner wagons.
> H = Hopper wagons.
> I = Internationally owned stock.
> J = Coil wagons.
> K = Coil wagons.
> M = Mineral wagons.
> O = Open goods wagons.
> R = Runner wagons, barrier wagons and diesel brake tenders.
> S = Non-bogie steel carrying wagons.
> U = Miscellaneous unconverted vacuum-braked wagon types.
> V = Vans.
> X = Specially constructed vehicles.
> Y = Departmental wagons.
> Z = Departmental wagons.

2. The second letter identifies which group the vehicle belongs to within its type.

3. The third letter indicates the type of braking the vehicle has viz:

> A = Air braked.
> B = Air braked with vacuum brake through pipe.
> O = Hand brake only.
> P = Vacuum brake through pipe.
> V = Vacuum braked.
> X = Dual air and vacuum brakes.

Wagon Labels - each wagon making a journey had to carry an appropriate label in a clip on the solebar. The label gave the date, sender, point of origin, destination, route, wagon letter and number, weight, description of load and consignee. *(see inside back cover)*

Plate 1. P202006 is a 13T, 7-plank wooden bodied side and end door open wagon originally owned by Parkhouse Collieries Ltd., Chesterton, Stoke on Trent. (Top of 'S' and 'on' visible on the bottom plank). The body was red oxide with white lettering shaded black. It has spindle buffers, split axleboxes and independent brakes. Seen here at Leamington Spa (GWR) station on 5th September, 1953.   H.F.W./R.C.

Plate 2. P386120 is an ex-Sutton Heath Collieries, Rainhill, Lancs 12T, 8-plank wooden bodied side and end door open coal wagon (end with end door is indicated by the white diagonal strapping on the body side). It has wooden solebars and headstock with iron fittings and has 2-shoe independent brakes. The original livery was grey body with white lettering shaded black and black ironwork - all this is very weathered in the photograph taken at Sidmouth on 26th August,1954.   H.F.W./R.C.

Plate 3. M58951 is a 13T, 7-plank wooden, side, end and bottom door wagon (the white 'V' indicates bottom door discharge facilities). It is an ex-Midland Railway wagon in 'wood' finish with white lettering on black patches, 'COND' indicates its days were numbered when it was photographed at Moreton-in-Marsh on 11th October,1958. It has open spoke wheels grease axleboxes, spindle buffers and 2 shoe independent brakes (necessary because of the bottom door discharge)

R.C.

Plate 4. B450847 is a 13T steel low goods wagon, diagram 1/002, lot No. 2194, (1000 vehicles, B450400 - B451399), vacuum braked and built at BR Shildon Works in 1951. Note the LNER-style eight shoe clasp brakes. The original classification 'LOWFIT' is just visible to the right of the wagon number. Photographed at Oxford Station on 5th September, 1979.

B.D.

Plate 5. 349948. A 13T, ex LMS, 2-plank open wagon with wooden body and headstocks but steel underframe and self contained buffers. One sided 2-shoe brakes made it an early candidate for scrapping. Livery was old LMS bauxite with white lettering. Built in 1913. Photographed in revenue earning service at St Albans City on 23rd May, 1949.   E.B.

Plate 6. B744755. A 30T steel hot pig iron wagon, diagram 1/005, lot No. 2857, (139 built B744621 - B744759) built at BR Shildon Works in 1956. Note the distorted body due to heat from the loads carried which also led to the 'weathered rust' livery (with white lettering).   G.E.

13

Plate 7. B459325 is a 13T steel medium goods wagon with drop sides, built to diagram 1/019, lot No. 2236, (1000 wagons B458597 - B459596) at BR Ashford Works in 1951. It has LMS style 8-shoe clasp vacuum brake gear with J hanger auxiliary suspension - all of which show up clearly in the ex-works photograph. Note also the chalk boards on the side and end and 'XP' indicating an 'express' rated wagon.   B.R./A.B.

Plate 8. DB459152 is a 13T steel medium goods wagon from the same diagram and lot as the previous photograph. It is here seen in departmental use (TOPS CODE ZAV) and has one pair of spoked wheels and one pair of disc wheels. Note the door controller above the V-hanger to assist in the lowering of the side and prevent injury. Photographed at Didcot, 6th January, 1980.   B.D.

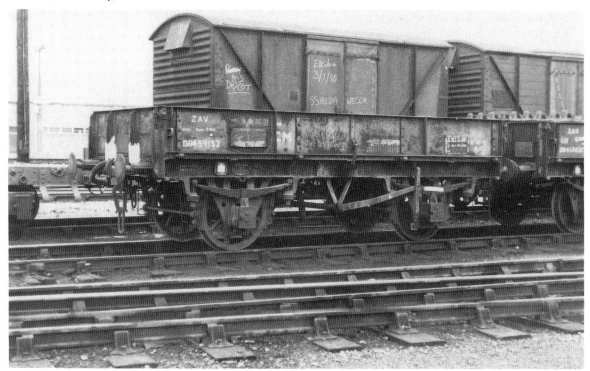

Plate 9. W140267 is an ex-GWR 5 plank open wagon with a steel chassis. It is unfitted and has Morton brake gear, split axleboxes, tie bars between the axleguards and has been fitted with Oleo replacement buffers, the housing of which is being used as rope anchors for the load. Note the prominent door bangers. Livery is weathered G.W. grey with white lettering.   C.C.

Plate 10. B483683. A 13T wooden bodied high goods wagon, side loading built to diagram 1/033, lot No. 2061, (1 lot of 100 vehicles B483650 - B483749) at BR Ashford Works in 1949. Note the new end - livery new/weathered wood with white lettering. Note door controllers, split axleboxes, spindle buffers and independent brakes.   G.E.

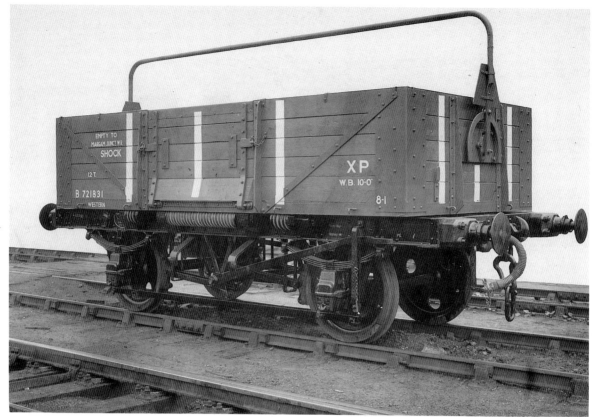

Plate 11. B721831 is a 12T shock absorbing high sided goods wagon with an all wooden body and steel sheet support rail, built to diagram 1/040, lot No. 2317, (600 wagons B721825 - B722424) at BR Derby Works in 1952. It has vacuum brakes, split axleboxes and tie bars. The shock absorbing springs are clearly visible just below the central door on the wagon side, (these springs were boarded over as a safety precaution - *see the next three photographs*). The white stripes on the bauxite body indicate that it is a shock absorbing wagon. It is designated to work from Margam Yard (near Swansea).
                                                                                                            B.R./A.B.

Plate 12. (AD)B723929 is a 12T shock absorbing high sided goods wagon, diagram 1/040, lot No. 2546, (250 wagons B723275 - B724024) built at BR Derby Works in 1955. It has similar details to the previous photograph except that the axleboxes are slightly different and it has corrugated steel ends. It is seen in departmental use having had several new planks added and also in need of another one!
                                                                                                            A.B.

Plate 13. B720382 is a 13T shock absorbing steel bodied wagon, vacuum braked to diagram 1/031, lot No. 2033, (175 vehicles B720250 - B720426) built at BR Shildon Works in 1949. It has LNER style 8-shoe clasp brakes and Duplex type spindle buffers. The small lettering reads 'RETURN TO BRIDGE ST, BRADFORD N.E.'   G.E.

Plate 14. B720969. 12T wooden bodied shock absorbing wagon, diagram 1/035, lot No. 2155, (300 vehicles B720925 - B721224), built at BR Ashford works in 1950. Note the vacuum pipe, screw couplings, tie bars and different buffers to the previous shock absorbing wagons shown.   G.E.

Plate 15. E296321. A 13T ex-LNER design all steel high sided goods wagon, express rated (XP), built at Darlington Works in 1948. Note the black chalk boards - which have been ignored. LNER pattern asymmetrical vacuum brake gear - vacuum pipe is black with grey hose. This LNER design was perpetuated by BR. Seen here at Lowestoft Fish Quay on 18th September, 1948.   E.B.

Plate 16. B496300. 13T high sided goods wagon with a steel body. Built to diagram 1/047, lot No. 2479, (650 vehicles B495970 - B496619) at BR Shildon Works in 1953. It shows that BR introduced changes to the LNER design, such as symmetrical vacuum brake gear, strengthened door and tie bars between axleguards. The bodyside dimples accommodate sheet hooks.   G.E.

Plate 17. B475529 was built as a 13T high sided goods wagon to diagram 1/037, lot No. 2128, (2000 vehicles B475050 - B477049) at BR Shildon Works in 1950. It has no tie bars but has split axleboxes and is fully fitted with LNER type brake gear. It has been modified to carry soda ash - a highly corrosive chemical (especially when wet) by the fitting of a sheet support rail and improved door fastenings. The small white lettering on the door reads, 'DOORS TO BE LOWERED WITH CARE' and to the right 'EMPTY TO DOWLOW SIDINGS, HINDLOW LMR(LNW).   B.D.

Plate 18. B556578 is a 16½ T end door all steel welded open wagon built to diagram 1/108, lot No. 2915, (TOPS Code MCV). This vacuum braked example of a common type of wagon was originally designated to sand traffic. It has 8-shoe clasp brakes, split axleboxes and oleo buffers.   G.E.

Plate 19. B746609 is a 13T steel sand wagon diagram 1/072, lot No. 2267, (250 wagons B746500 - B746749 - one lot only) built at BR Swindon Works in 1951. It is unfitted with Morton brakes, three link couplings and spindle buffers. Many of these wagons had return destinations printed on the sides, when new - Leighton Buzzard and Congleton being two common ones.   B.R./A.B.

Plate 20. B746426. A 13T open sand wagon, diagram 1/071, lot No. 2157 (one lot only of 500 wagons B746000 - B746499) built at BR Ashford Works in 1950, vacuum braked. The wagon in this photograph is surrounded by Prestwin cement wagons - a type which followed the Presflo - but only forty were built.   G.E.

Plate 21. 17193 is an ex-GWR 10T match truck - a very short wheelbase wagon used for running under an overhanging load but could take a load on its own. No chains or beams were provided and to secure a load, large wooden chocks would be nailed to the floor of the wagon and then the load roped. Livery - weathered GWR grey with white lettering. Note the diagram 1/112 MOS cupboard door mineral wagon in the background built originally c1946 for service on the SNCF in France but later repatriated and seen here at Brockenhurst on 11th June, 1964.   H.F.W./R.C.

Plate 22. 39498 is an ex-GWR Conflat 12T, diagram H7, lot No. 1188, built between 1933 and 1939 and is vacuum braked. It still carries weathered GW livery (grey with white lettering). The central section reads 'To be retained for G.W. Containers. Chain pocket lids to be replaced after chains have been removed'. Type A container, 3T and numbered A1312, diagram 3/001, lot No. 2436 (235 units A1311 - A1345B), built at BR Wolverton Works in 1953 and finished in bauxite with white lettering, seen here at St Albans City on 15th May, 1949.   E.B.

Plate 23. B738545 is a 14T Container wagon - 'CONFLAT L' diagram 1/064, lot No. 2489 (one lot only of 373 wagons B738500 - B738872) built at BR Ashford works in 1953. It is vacuum braked and is fitted with tie bars, plate front axleboxes and spoked wheels. Note the shallow hinged sides and ends, wagon plate, label holder and label, couplings and instructions printed on the side.
B.R./A.B.

Plate 24. B702326 is an 11T container flat wagon (CONFLAT A), diagram 1/067, lot No. 2853, (1000 vehicles B701500 - B702499) built at BR Ashford Works in 1956. It has split spoked wheels and is vacuum braked. The BD container No. 2211W is of GWR origin, 4 tons capacity with side and end doors. These containers were painted in GWR brown, with yellow lettering initially, but in later years they were painted red with cream lettering - a style similar to that adopted by BR. It was built in 1941 and is seen here at Burton on Trent on 12th April, 1957.
W.C.

Plate 25. M70712 is an ex-LMS 10T diagram D2035 vacuum fitted chassis for the road/rail beer tanks (CODE TUF) built at Derby Works in 1939. One of four in the lot, it has 10ft wheelbase and now has four disc wheels and BR plate front axleboxes as well as the board with the two white stars on (they were originally painted on the side of the road tank guide rails). Livery here was black solebars and below, with bauxite edge to the floor and above as well as the end over the buffers. Lettering was in white - that along the body edge reads 'FOR USE OF WHITBREADS TANKS ONLY'. The 4-wheeled road tank is one of a type originally used for carrying milk but later brewers were encouraged to use them when they were often painted in the brewery colours. Note the drawbar details of the tank and the chain with turnbuckles which anchor it. Photographed on display at Birmingham Central Goods Depot in 1959.   R.C.

Plate 26. B709827 is a 12T container flat wagon lettered 'CONFLAT A' (TOPS Code FAV), diagram 1/069, lot No. 3084 (250 vehicles B709700 - B709949) built at BR Wolverton Works in 1958. Originally rated at 13 tons, these wagons were vacuum braked and this one has had Oleo buffers fitted. The load is a BR plate backed bogie as typically fitted to the Bogie Bolster 'C' type wagons. Photographed at Temple Mills on 13th September, 1979.   B.D.

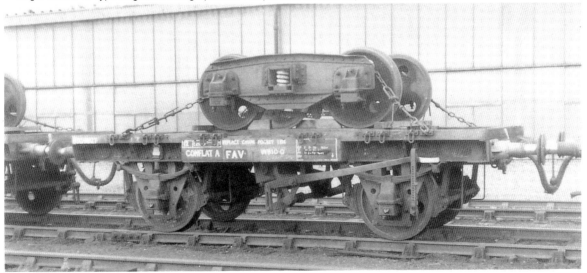

Plate 27. B493421. 13T 5-plank high sided goods wagon with wooden body and corrugated ends(TOPS Code OWV) diagram 1/044, lot No. 2396,(1200 vehicles B492700 - B493899), built in 1951 by Gloucester Carriage and Wagon Co Ltd. It has a sheet rail fitted and plate front axleboxes. The vacuum brake pipe and instanter couplings are clearly visible but there is little sign of the original bauxite paint on the body. The white lettering has been applied on black patches when seen here at Temple Mills in November, 1979.   B.D.

Plate 28. 129246 is an ex-GWR, 13T 5-plank wooden open wagon, diagram O32, lot No. 1123. New planking has almost obliterated the 'G' but the 'W' remains as does the original painting of the wagon number.'W13T' has been added where the 'W' should have been painted before the wagon numbers. Livery is weathered GW grey with white lettering. The load is of interest being the cab sides, cut down to the bottom of the side windows, from the single LNER class B3/3, 4-6-0 locomotive introduced in 1943 (a Thompson rebuild of a Robinson Great Central B3/2) which was withdrawn in 1949.   R.C.

Plate 29. M424453. A 13T 5-plank open wagon of LMS design, although built post Nationalisation, at BR Derby Works. Like many vehicles built just post-war, it was outshopped unpainted except for white lettering printed on black patches. Body ironwork was painted in red oxide but the solebars and below were in black. It has two shoe brakes on one side only. Photographed at Radlett on 26th February, 1949.   E.B.

Plate 30. DE281493. This is a 13T high sided goods wagon from the series 280209 to 283208, built by the LNER just before Nationalisation. (A second batch 293145 - 296844 were still being built at Nationalisation when some 3,562 wagons, to this design were in traffic). It is as built except for plate-front axleboxes and is seen at Didcot in departmental use; TOPS Code ZGO.   B.D.

Plate 31. 5362 is a 13T all steel mineral wagon produced by the Butterley Company as a private development to replace the wooden bodied wagons. It has an end door, riveted body, spilt axleboxes, independent brake gear (hence the double V hangers) and was finished in bauxite with white lettering. Seen here at St Albans City on 15th April, 1949.

E.B.

Plate 32. B39649 is a 16T end door wagon to diagram 1/103 - one of a batch of 1572 wagons (B39501 - B41072) built by Metro Cammell in 1948 and registered by the LMS - being taken into BR stock soon after completion it was given a 'B' prefix number. It has a 9ft wheelbase with independent double Morton brakes - both characteristic of the 'pre-1948' built wagons of this type. Other features include split axleboxes, spindle buffers and a rivetted body with no top door on the sides.

G.E.

Plate 33. B 595425 is a 16T end door wagon diagram 1/108, lot No. 3063, (350 wagons B595150 - B595499) built in 1957 by the Derbyshire Wagon Co. It has a welded steel body with top side door but the end door is pressed. It has 8 shoe clasp vacuum brakes with slotted link brake gear. Other features include split axleboxes, screw couplings, self contained buffers but no tie bars. *Note:* This diagram produced 20,644 wagons between 1950 and 1959. Variations were common including:- different buffers; different axle guards; welded body/ riveted body; fitted/ unfitted; top doors on the side/ no top doors; tie bars/ no tie bars. *Plates 33 - 39* show some of these differences listed above.   A.B.

Plate 34. B252077 is a 16T end door wagon with all steel welded body, diagram 1/108, lot No. 2748 (2000 wagons B253609 - B255608) built in 1956 by Metro Cammell. It is unfitted and has split axleboxes, spindle buffers, Morton brakegear and top doors on the sides.   P.B.

Plate 35. 041680, ex-B257698 is a 16T end door wagon with steel welded body built to diagram 1/108, lot No. 2802, (1000 wagons B257609 - B258608) by the Teeside Bridge and Engineering Co in 1956. It is unfitted with Morton brake gear (brakes are on one side only) plate front axleboxes, standard spindle buffers and is fitted with a top side door. Note the prominent door banger to prevent damage to the V-hanger when the side door is opened. It was in internal use when photographed at Stratford Depot in 1989 and is in heavily rusted very light grey (including solebar) livery.

T.R.

Plate 36. B241057 built to lot No. 2389 (2000 vehicles, B241009 - B243008) by Birmingham Railway Carriage and Wagon Co Ltd in 1959; has a pressed end door with a welded body, top door to sides and is unfitted but shows one of the more subtle variations here with one plate front axlebox and one split axlebox.

G.E.

Plate 37. B561542 is a 16T end door wagon, diagram 1/108, lot No. 2918 (1000 wagons B561200 - B562199) built in 1957 by R.Y.Pickering & Co. It has split axleboxes and tie bars but has been re-bodied and fitted with vacuum brakes. Coded MCV its livery is weathered rusty bauxite. A.B.

Plate 38. B261632 built to lot No. 2806 (206 wagons B261509 - B261714) by Cambrian Wagon Works in 1957 - one of only 12 lots out of 93 lots to diagram 1/108 to be vacuum braked. It has a riveted body, top side doors and self contained buffers. G.E.

Plate 39. B229637 built to lot No. 2745 (700 wagons B229309 - B230008) by Derbyshire Wagon Co in 1955. Unfitted, split axleboxes, Morton brakes and it has been re-bodied. (TOPS Code MCO). Seen here at Workington on 3rd September, 1979.

B.D.

Plate 40. DB558375 is a 16T end door wagon , diagram 1/117, lot No. 3146 (1000 wagons B557750 - B558749) built by Pressed Steel in 1958. It has eight shoe clasp vacuum brakes, split axleboxes and replacement Oleo buffers. It has also been re-bodied - note the curved bottom to the bodyside and absence of the top door on the sides. Livery was 'weathered rust' when photographed at Toton in 1989.

T.R.

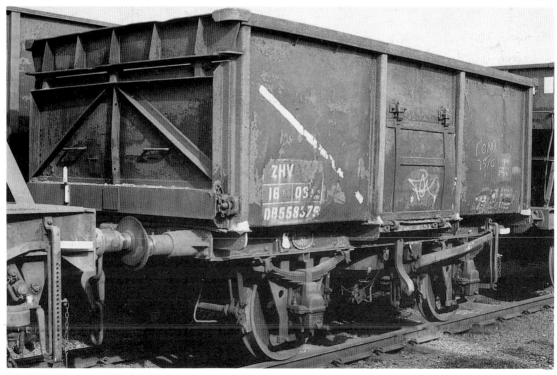

Plate 41. DW83119 is a 20T ex-GWR locomotive coal wagon built to diagram N22, lot No. 902 in 1923/24. It is of riveted construction and has Dean-Churchward brake gear, tie rod, spoked wheels and heavy duty buffers. It is finished in light grey all over with white lettering on black patches and seen here at Machynlleth in August 1951.   N.

Plate 42. W33387 is a 20T ex-GWR locomotive coal wagon to diagram N28. It has a riveted body with later brake and tie bars; livery is as on the previous photograph but here we have black solebars and below. Split axleboxes, disc wheels and the two diagonal white stripes indicate the unusual feature of end doors at both ends of this wagon.1959.

R.C.

Plate 43. E300531. A 21T ex-LNER locomotive coal wagon with an all steel body fitted with cupboard-type doors. Built at Darlington in 1948, it is finished in grey with white lettering. LNER axleboxes and 4-shoe brake gear along with tie bars and spoked wheels. Photographed at Hatfield on 4th March, 1950. E.B.

Plate 44. B201689 is a 21T end door wagon of all steel construction with a welded body built to diagram 1/107, lot No. 2192 (500 wagons B201500 - B201999) by Charles Roberts in 1950. It is unfitted with plate front axleboxes and tie bars. This design was really a larger wheelbase and slightly higher version of the more common diagram 1/108 - in this case lacking top flap doors to the sides. B.R./A.B.

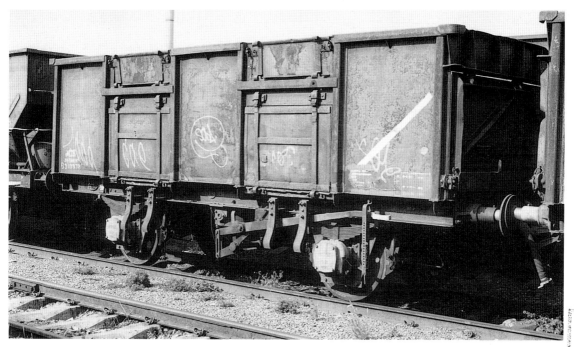

Plate 45. B310372 is an all steel welded 21T mineral wagon to diagram 1/119, lot No. 3307 (1000 wagons B310000 - B310999) built at BR Shildon Works in 1961. It is fitted with manual change over vacuum brakes and hydraulic buffers. When originally built it had roller bearing axleboxes but when photographed at Toton in the 1980's, it had been fitted with Hybox axleboxes and the livery at that time was rusty grey.   T.R.

Plate 46. B313014 is a 21T mineral wagon to the later diagram 1/120, lot No. 3430 (1500 wagons B312000 - B313499) built at BR Derby Works in 1962 (CODED MDV). It is fitted with S.A.B. vacuum brakes and has roller bearings and hydraulic buffers but there are no tie bars between the axleguards. The later 21T wagons had flaps over the side doors. Livery is well rusted bauxite which has almost obliterated the small lettering at the top of the left hand side.   T.R.

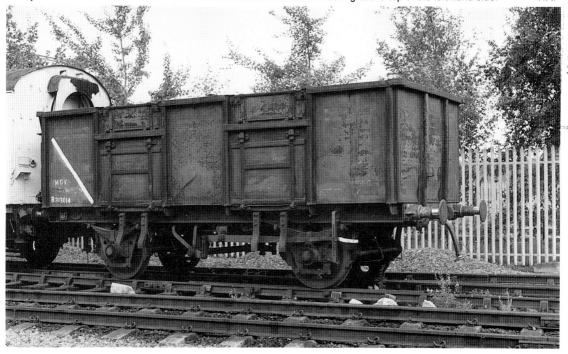

Plate 47. B282742. A 24½T side and end doors coal wagon fitted with roller bearings and self contained buffers, built to diagram 1/118, lot No. 3244 (620 wagons B282150 - B282769) at BR Ashford Works in 1959. Instanter couplings, tie bar and door bangers are prominent on this unfitted wagon.   B.D.

Plate 48. B200686 is a 21½T steel bodied mineral wagon built originally to diagram 1/110, lot No. 2190 (one lot only of 1,000 vehicles B200000 - B200999) by Metro Cammell in 1950. These wagons had an end door and riveted body but some were rebuilt c1977 with no end doors and only one side door to the left. No later diagram number was issued (TOPS Code MDO). To compound the problems of these rebuilds, they were unfitted but were finished in bauxite with white lettering.   B.D.

Plate 49. A view taken from the train on 13th June, 1950 of Whitehaven Colliery, Cumbria showing several varieties of ex-NE type 13T and 20T wooden-bodied hopper wagons now in internal National Coal Board use. Note the massive end posts which extend below the headstocks for use with Chaldron wagons. These posts were cut off at the bottom of the headstocks by the LNER from 1925 *(see plate 52).*

E.B.

Plate 50. E189453. A 13T ex-LNER, 8-plank coal hopper wagon of all wooden construction with steel fittings, registered at Doncaster in 1936 but built by G.R.Turner, Langley Mill (right hand plate on the solebar). Still showing relics of the LNER grey finish with white lettering (new lettering is on a black patch). It has T-end stanchions, self contained buffers on a new headstock and is fitted with a one-sided two shoe brake system. Seen here in company with BR 20T steel hopper wagon B410771 at North Blythe on 17th May, 1958. R.C.

Plate 51. E243921 is a 13T ex-LNER coal hopper based on the NE 12T design (built at Darlington in 1941), but having the bottom two planks sloping inwards. Body/headstocks/solebars are all wooden with steel fittings. Various new planks can be seen, the others have had a coat of dark grey paint - lettering is white. E41229, a 20T ex-LNER coal hopper wagon of NE origin (LNER built hoppers had T-section end posts). Plain wood finish with white lettering on black painted patches and seen here at North Blythe on 17th May, 1958. R.C.

Plate 52. P61140. A 13T ex-private owner/NE wooden hopper wagon in weathered wood finish with white lettering on black patches. Note 'V' with 'HOPPER' above indicating bottom discharge. The lettering on the panel top left reads 'LOAD ONLY TO BEA, EAST MIDLAND DIVISION, POWER STATIONS'. It was obviously in need of care and attention when photographed at North Blythe on 17th May, 1958, hence the chalked message 'Travel next to van' (brakevan).   R.C.

Plate 53. B400048 is a 13T HOP13 steel bodied coal hopper wagon with wooden bottom doors (as built). Diagram 1/142, lot No. 2038 (200 wagons B400000 - B400199) built at BR Shildon Works in 1949. Note the self contained buffers, brakes on one side only (operable from both sides), open spoked wheels and unfitted.   G.E.

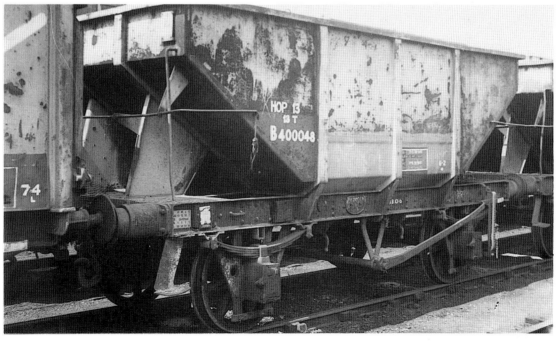

Plate 54. E302077. A 21½T ex-LNER coal hopper (TOPS Code HTO) originally built by Metro-Cammell in 1947 and registered at Darlington, it was rebuilt with a welded body at BR Shildon Works in 1977 when it was turned out in bauxite livery with white lettering (despite being unfitted) and seen here at Chinnor, Oxon on 28th December, 1978.

G.G.

Plate 55. E205893. A 21½T ex-LNER all steel bodied coal hopper wagon built by Hurst Nelson, Motherwell in 1937 and registered by the LNER at Darlington, seen here at Chinnor, Oxon on 28th December, 1978. Two-shoe brakes on one side only - note the high off position of the brake lever - unfitted.

G.G.

Plate 56. B413317 is a 21T hopper coal wagon with riveted body, diagram 1/143, lot No. 2168 (450 wagons B413250 - B413699) built by Head Wrightson in 1950 (TOPS CODE HTO). Unfitted but with clasp brakes and plate front axleboxes. Photographed at Chinnor, Oxon on 28th December, 1978.   G.G.

Plate 57. B414029 is a 21T all steel welded hopper coal wagon built to diagram 1/146, lot No. 2330 (100 wagons B413950 - B414049) at BR Shildon Works in November 1952. It has tie bars, 20T standard hand lever brake. 16,800 wagons were built to this diagram between 1952 and 1959.   B.R./A.B.

Plate 58. E274116. A 21T ex-LNER all steel bodied coal hopper wagon with welded six-panel body (CODE HOP21). Unfitted, with brakes on one side only and the high brake lever, plus plate front axleboxes. Photographed at Temple Mills on 13th September, 1979. B.D.

Plate 59. B422686 is a 21T welded steel bodied coal hopper wagon built to diagram 1/146, lot No. 3013 (500 wagons B422250 - B422749) by Fairfields in 1957. It features roller bearing axle boxes, tie bars and standard brake gear but is unfitted. G.E.

Plate 60. B432987K. A 21T coal hopper wagon with a welded body, diagram 1/146, lot No. 3157 (2950 vehicles B430800 - B433749) built by Pressed Steel in 1958. It was vacuum fitted with roller bearings, spindle buffers and tie bars and bears the legend 'HOUSE COAL CONCENTRATION' being dedicated to carrying coal to the large mechanised depots when small coal yards closed down. G.E.

Plate 61. 352487 is a 32½T coal hopper wagon (TOPS Code HAA) to design code HA002K, lot No. 3574 built at BR Shildon Works in 1966/69. These wagons formed an early part of the 1960's re-design policy by having a longer wheelbase than previous coal hoppers, plus being air braked. Many actually carried a 'B' code number - the only air braked wagons to do so - in this case the 'B' has not been painted although it is on the cast wagon plate. B.D.

Plate 62. B885024 is a 20T grain hopper wagon built to diagram 1/270, lot No.2009, (40 wagons in one lot only B885000 - B885039) at BR Derby Works in 1949, to an LMS design. All steel riveted body with roller bearings and tie bars, unfitted. G.E.

Plate 63. B885383 is a 20T grain hopper wagon with all steel welded body built to diagram 1/271, lot No. 2925 (100 wagons B885310 - B885409) by Pressed Steel Ltd in 1956 (TOPS Code CGO) - an unfitted wagon with roller bearing axleboxes and tie bars fitted because brakes only apply to the outside of the four wheels to clear the bottom discharge facility. B.D.

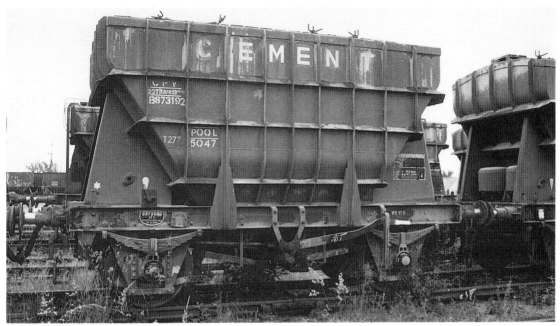

Plate 64. B873192 is the penultimate 21T Presflo hopper cement wagon of diagram 1/272, lot No. 3323 (170 wagons B873024 - B873193) built by the Gloucester Carriage and Wagon Company Ltd. in 1960. Classified CPV in the 1980's when photographed in Salisbury Yard, it was vacuum braked and has roller bearing axleboxes. The livery is weathered black solebars and below with brown body and stays.   T.R.

Plate 65. B887982 is a 20T hopper cement wagon, PRESFLO CEMENT (TOPS Code CPV) built to diagram 1/272, lot No. 3177 (200 wagons B887800 - B887999) by Gloucester Carriage and Wagon Co Ltd in 1958, seen here at Temple Mills on 13th August, 1979. These special bulk powder carriers were vacuum braked and some were used to carry alumina and were so lettered instead of 'cement'.   B.D.

Plate 66. B873804. A 22T hopper cement wagon RUGBY CEMENT built to diagram 1/272, lot No. 3497 (100 wagons B873794 - B873893) by the Central Wagon Co Ltd in 1964. This view at Temple Mills on 14th September, 1979, shows the operating gear for the discharge of the cement (to the left of the V hanger). Vacuum braked, it is finished in standard bauxite livery but 'RUGBY CEMENT' is black on an orange board. (TOPS Code CPV). 		B.D.

Plate 67. B874169. 21T fly-ash wagon, design code CS002C, lot No. 3663, built at BR Ashford Works in 1968 (TOPS Code CSA). These air braked Presflos were built to convey fly-ash (ash waste from power stations) to various bulk users. They are finished in bauxite with black solebars and below, lettering being white. 		B.D.

Plate 68. B336937N is a 24½T coal hopper wagon built to diagram 1/148, lot No. 3437 (243 wagons B336933 - B337175). Built at BR Shildon Works in 1962, these unfitted wagons replaced the 24½T mineral wagons on power station workings and this wagon was dedicated to 'LOAD ONLY TO THORPE MARSH POWER STATION (YORKS) NER' (as the lettering reads on the top left). It has roller bearing axleboxes, tie bars, self contained buffers and a long brake lever - the V-hanger being displaced due to bottom discharge. G.E.

Plate 69. B449170 is a 20T hopper coke wagon built to diagram 1/152, lot No. 3122 (550 wagons in one lot only B448650 - B449199) at BR Shildon works in 1958. These wagons had no raves (top side/end rails) but full height sheeting on both sides and ends. Some were welded like this one, some were riveted, some were fitted and some (like this one) were unfitted. Features include roller bearings, tie bars and two shoe brakes on each side - the reversing linkage for the nearside brake lever is clearly seen. G.E.

Plate 70. B447057, a 20T hopper coke wagon built to diagram 1/150, lot No. 2039 (400 wagons B447000 - B447399) at BR Shildon Works in 1949 and fitted with both end and side raves. It is of riveted construction, unfitted with plain axleboxes and tie bar. Brakes are similar to the previous wagon. G.E.

Plate 71. B438510 is a 25½T hopper sand wagon built to diagram 1/163, lot No.2733 (900 wagons B438000 - B438899) at BR Shildon Works in 1955 as an ironstone hopper wagon. It has self contained buffers, plate front axleboxes and tie bars. The small lettering gives instructions about bottom door opening and closing. G.E.

Plate 72. B747092 is a 25T hopper anhydrite wagon built to diagram 1/179, lot No. 2597 (150 wagons in one lot B747000 - B747149) at BR Shildon Works in 1954. Vacuum braked, with 8 shoe clasp brakes, roller bearings and self contained buffers. These wagons were dedicated to working the 'Long Meg' mineral trains which carried anhydrite rock from quarries on the Settle and Carlisle line to Widnes in Cheshire, where it was used in the manufacture of sulphuric acid.   G.E.

Plate 73. B439758, a 24T hopper wagon built to diagram 1/166, lot No. 3189 (350 wagons in one lot B437500 - B437899) at BR Shildon Works in 1957 - originally built as a 25½T vacuum braked ironstone hopper wagon, here in modified form for Limestone Traffic. The wagon plate reads B439758 but the number on the bodyside is B429758 !

G.E.

Plate 74. B870688, a 24½T covered hopper wagon built to diagram 1/210, lot No. 3431 (130 wagons B870630 - B870759) at BR Ashford Works in 1961 (Code COVHOP VP). This was one of four lots to have vacuum pipes but normal brakes, however it carried bauxite livery with white lettering. The 'BIS Sand for Rockware Glass Ltd' is in white paint on a black band (from the angle of the body to just below the bottom of the central overhead wires indicator label). This hopper, seen here at Kings Lynn on 25th August, 1977, was dedicated to carrying high quality sand from Middleton Towers, near Kings Lynn to glassworks in Yorkshire.   G.G.

Plate 75. B886291. A 24T covered hopper wagon built to diagram 1/120, lot No. 2767 (50 wagons B886262 - B886311) at BR Derby Works in 1955 - unfitted and coded CHO. Note the 'dashed box' numbering. It was dedicated to carrying corrosive soda ash. The instructions are painted in white on the central black panel and relate to how to open the bottom hopper doors from this side of the wagon. Photographed at Workington on 3rd September, 1979.   B.D.

Plate 76. B931211 is a 22T plate wagon built to diagram 1/431, lot No. 2199 (540 wagons B931050 - B931589) at BR Shildon Works in 1951. It is unfitted with plate front axleboxes. To the right of it can be seen part of wagon B934307 built to diagram 1/434, lot No. 3223 (1500 wagons B934025 - B935524) at BR Shildon Works in 1959, which is fitted and has isothermos axleboxes when seen here at Sutton Bridge Junction on 15th April, 1964.   N.

Plate 77. B931972 is a 22T plate wagon built to diagram 1/431, lot No. 2476 (225 wagons B931750 - B931974) at BR Shildon Works in 1953. It has plate front axleboxes, tie bars and the standard 20T (or long link) brakes.   B.R./A.B.

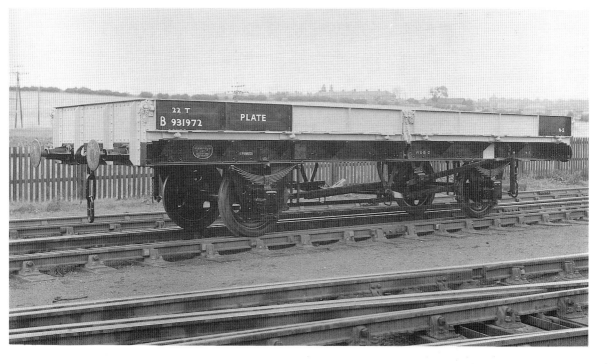

Plate 78. CDB935056 is a 22T plate wagon diagram 1/434, lot No. 3223 (1500 wagons B934025 - B935524) built at BR Shildon Works in 1959. It has 8 shoe clasp vacuum brakes with slotted link brakegear, pneumatic buffers and roller bearing axleboxes. The body is showing signs of wear when photographed at Hoo Junction in the 1980's.   T.R.

Plate 79. B935972 started life as a 22T plate wagon built to diagram 1/434, lot No. 3338 (1000 wagons B935525 - B936524) at BR Shildon Works in 1961. It is vacuum braked with eight shoe clasp brakes and has Hybox axleboxes. It is no longer a plate wagon but has been given corner and end stanchions along with side rails to form two cradles to carry coils of steel wire as seen here (TOPS Code KRV)   B.D.

Plate 80. E312490 is a 13T rod in coil wagon, diagram 1/450 (CODE 'COILS' then KSV). This wagon was one of several conversions from LNER diagrams 185 and 210 'Highfits'/'Hyfits' in which the solebars and below remained largely unaltered, (new buffers have been fitted here) and the lower body side plank was retained as were the planks between the centre end stanchions. Two parallel racks were built on the deck to take the coiled rod. B.D.

Plate 81. B382254 is a 27T 'COIL J' wagon - formerly a 27T iron ore wagon (tippler) built to diagram 1/183, lot No. 2498, which has had its sides and ends reduced in height but is still unfitted and basically the same as built from the solebars downwards. It is seen in its new guise carrying coils of sheet steel. G.E.

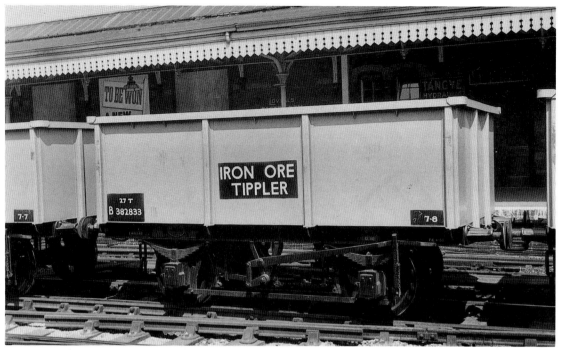

Plate 82. B382833, a 27T iron ore tippler wagon built to diagram 1/183, lot No. 2498 (240 wagons B381900 - B383139) at BR Shildon Works in 1953. It has plate front axleboxes, tie bars, independent two shoe brake gear and is unfitted - seen here in ex-works livery at Gloucester on 9th May, 1953.   E.B.

Plate 83. E253564 is a 21T ex-LNER rivetted iron ore hopper wagon built by G.R.Turner and registered by the LNER in 1941, seen here at Tebay Yard on 29th May, 1952. It has a long ornate brake lever on both sides but brakes only on one side. Note the long stock buffers with access slots and it is unfitted.   E.B.

Plate 84. B445319, a 33T iron ore hopper wagon 'ORE HOP VB', built to diagram 1/164, lot No. 2962 (one lot of 270 wagons B445150 - B445419) at BR Shildon Works in 1956. It is a fitted wagon with clasp type brakes, plate front axleboxes and buffers similar to the wagon in *plate 83*.　　　　　　　　　　　　　　　　　　　　G.E.

Plate 85. B439991 is a 24T iron ore hopper wagon 'ORE HOP VB', built to diagram 1/166, lot No. 3189 (one lot of 350 wagons B439700 - B440049) at BR Shildon Works in 1959. It is a fitted wagon with roller bearings and later pattern brake gear compared to the previous wagon. Note the difference in shapes of the hopper bodies.　　　　　　　　G.E.

Plate 86. B384378 is a 27T iron ore wagon, originally lettered 'Iron Ore Tippler' and built to diagram 1/183, lot No. 2730 (1500 wagons B383640 - B385139) at BR Shildon Works in 1953. It has tie bars and two different types of roller bearings. It is an unfitted vehicle with extra livery details where the top angle of the body and the patch on which INGOT MOULD is painted, are yellow - the latter letters are black. In this guise, seen here at Workington on 3rd September, 1979, it was used to carry large pieces of steel, which rode on a bed of gravel on the floor of the wagon.

B.D.

Plate 87. B387604 is a 27T iron ore tippler wagon built to diagram 1/183, lot No. 3324 (1000 wagons B387090 - B399089) at BR Derby Works in 1960, but here in use for stone traffic from quarries in the Frome area of Somerset to Bracknell in Berkshire - a terminal for stone for use in motorway construction.

G.E.

Plate 88. DB385955 is a 27T iron ore wagon originally lettered 'Iron Ore Tippler' on the central side panel, built to diagram 1/184, lot No. 3091 (420 wagons B385670 - B387089) at BR Derby Works in 1958. It is here coded ZKV and is in use as a ballast wagon by the Engineers department when photographed at Bristol Temple Meads in 1993. Its original features remain however - it has Timken (left) and SKF (right) roller bearings, Oleo buffers and is vacuum braked. The livery is 'weathered rust'.   T.R.

Plate 89. B386523, a 27T iron ore tippler wagon with build details as for *plate 88*. These wagons had bodies similar to diagram 1/108 but had no side or end doors being designed to be unloaded at sites with tippling facilities. It is fitted with SKF roller bearings, vacuum brakes and Oleo buffers. 7637 is its pool number being latterly dedicated to STONE traffic (the 'STONE' has been painted out on the top right of the bodyside). Because of its intensive use the Preventive Maintenance date (PM) is given in the number panel, '9-11-79' when photographed at Didcot in November, 1979.   B.D.

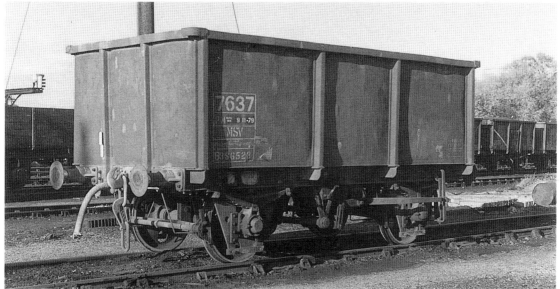

Plate 90. B933061 was originally built to diagram 1/432, lot No. 2734 (550 wagons B932825 - B933374) at BR Shildon Works in 1955 as a vacuum braked 22T plate wagon, it has been converted to carry timber and paper pulp via an earlier conversion to a Conflat P. It has roller bearings, Oleo buffers and was coded UUV. These wagons were used principally on the West Highland line and this view was taken at Crianlarich on 1st September, 1979.   B.D.

Plate 91. B455531 is a 15T vacuum braked open timber truck built to diagram 1/420, lot No. 3465 (1 lot of 80 wagons B455500 - B455579) at BR Ashford Works in 1962. It has 8-shoe clasp brakes, slotted link brake gear, roller bearing axleboxes and Oleo type buffers.   G.E.

Plate 92. B731490 is a 22T tube wagon built to diagram 1/447, lot No. 2457 (100 wagons B731490 - B731589) at BR Wolverton Works in 1953 - the first wagon of this lot. In this official photograph the bodysides have only had grey paint applied to the planks where black numbering patches are painted plus the strapping. This design was basically of LMS style (diagram No. 2116). It has an RCH long link unfitted underframe with a 17 feet 6 inches wheelbase. Note the small drop door on the side and corrugated steel end with chalkboard.   B.R./A.B.

Plate 93. B732256, a 22T tube wagon (coded STV) built to diagram 1/448, lot No. 2740 (350 wagons B732040 - B733289) at BR Faverdale Works, Darlington in 1955. Based on a wagon design used by the LNER, this wagon was 32 feet long, had corrugated ends, plate front axleboxes, early pattern buffers and was vacuum braked with 8 shoe clasp brakes.   B.D.

Plate 94. ADB733136 is a 22T tube wagon diagram 1/448, lot No. 3226 (180 wagons B733040 - B733219) built at BR Faverdale Works, Darlington in 1959. This BR revised design of diagram 1/447 had an 18ft 6ins wheelbase, 8 shoe clasp type vacuum brake gear and roller bearing axleboxes. This wagon has had new buffers fitted when photographed at Tonbridge West Yard in 1993. It is coded ZDV and is in use as a general materials carrier for the Engineers department.   T.R.

Plate 95. B733223 is a 22T tube wagon built to diagram 1/449, lot No. 3258 (20 wagons in one lot B733220 - B733239) at BR Faverdale Works, Darlington in 1959. Coded OIX, the anchor symbol indicates that this wagon is for Continental traffic use which is what these vehicles were originally built for. It is 32 feet long and has corrugated ends and wooden sides but other features are very different from *plate 93*. These include doors, RIV oval type self contained buffers, dual (vacuum/air) brakes, RIV link suspension, roller bearing axleboxes and different style handbrake lever.   B.D.

Plate 96. B740741. 13T pipe wagon (coded SOV) built diagram 1/460, lot No. 2458 (200 wagons B740700 - B740899) at BR Wolverton Works in 1953. This design was derived from an LNER wagon type used to carry pipes from the Stanton & Staveley Works. Seen here at Oxford on 5th September, 1979, it has 4 shoe vacuum brakes, split axleboxes, tie bars.Note the lamp iron on the end. B.D.

Plate 97. KDB741799 was originally built as a 12T pipe wagon lettered: Pipefit, to diagram 1/462, lot No. 3335 (200 wagons B741750 - B741949) at BR Wolverton Works in 1961. It has BR clasp type vacuum brake gear with a short ornate brake lever, the original plate front axleboxes and has had some new planking painted red oxide but the buffers are replacements. Photographed at Bristol Temple Meads in 1993. T.R.

Plate 98. B730669 is a 22T ale pallet wagon - originally built in 1965 to diagram 1/448, lot No. 3288 as a 22T tube wagon. It is vacuum braked and has Hybox axleboxes. These wagons were produced to carry metal kegs of beer on wooden pallets which were loaded through the doors all along the side. G.E.

Back cover top left:
B431111 - a 21T Hopper Coal wagon, diagram 1/146, lot No. 3157 - the largest lot being 2,950 vehicles (B430800 - B433749). It was built in 1958 by Pressed Steel and is seen here on 9th April, 1986, bearing the letter classification HTV at Chinnor Cement Works with a load of powdered coal for use in cement production. G.G.

Back cover top right:
B743470 - a 13T wooden bodied China Clay wagon with end door, built at Swindon in 1958 to diagram 1/051, lot No. 3098 (175 vacuum braked vehicles, B743400 - B743574). Used to transport china clay from Cornwall to the Potteries. They were originally sheeted but later (as here) fitted with a 'hood'. The bauxite livery is just apparent and in the TOPS coding carried the letters UCV. Seen here at St Blazey on 24th July, 1980. B.D.

Back cover bottom left:
B734059 - a 14T Conflat A with three containers used for carrying cement in a way which preceded the Presflo wagon. Built in 1955 at Swindon Works and seen here at Temple Mills on 8th June, 1980 is one of 300 vehicles to diagram 1/068, lot No. 2764 (B734000 - B734299) which were vacuum braked B.D.

Back cover bottom right:
B461224 - a 13T medium goods wagon of diagram 1/019, lot No.2488 (600 built to numbers B460997 - B461596) constructed at Ashford Works in 1952. It is vacuum braked and photographed in April, 1991. B.D.